❧ F O R ❧

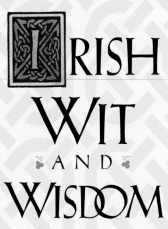

IRISH WIT AND WISDOM

By JOAN LARSON KELLY

DESIGN BY MULLEN & KATZ

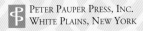

PETER PAUPER PRESS, Inc.
WHITE PLAINS, NEW YORK

IRISH WIT
AND
WISDOM

Contents

Introduction 5

Blarney 8

Folklore 11

Fairies—Fair and Foul . . . 15

Irish Humor 24

Proverbs and Sayings 45

Irish Sayings 54

Limericks 56

Toasts 62

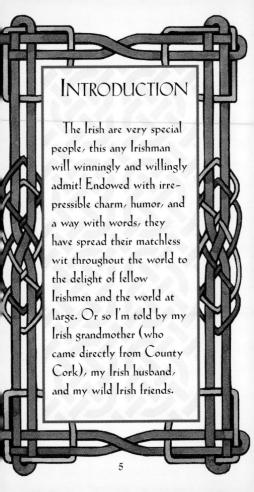

INTRODUCTION

The Irish are very special people, this any Irishman will winningly and willingly admit! Endowed with irrepressible charm, humor, and a way with words, they have spread their matchless wit throughout the world to the delight of fellow Irishmen and the world at large. Or so I'm told by my Irish grandmother (who came directly from County Cork), my Irish husband, and my wild Irish friends.

Perhaps no other country has spawned such a wealth of legends, stories, and story tellers as Ireland. Indeed the Irish are *masters* of the art of story telling. And why not? For centuries their major pastime was sitting around a turf fire sharpening their wits and outdoing each other in story telling and joking.

Irish people have the ability to look upon life as a show, and not a few of them see themselves as the star performer. Conversation is a game of wit Irishmen delight in playing.

True wit is highly respected. Anyone, they believe, can be witty. The true test of wit is when the odds are against you. To be witty then assures you of immortality.

The power of words, like wit, is greatly admired. If the words rhyme so much the better. Indeed poets of bygone days ranked above warriors in the courts of Gaelic kings.

No Irishman seems to lack imagination.

Coupled with a flair for the mystical, it is no wonder that the country has produced, over the centuries, superb fairy tales. The truth of the matter is that the Irish have never really stopped believing in fairies, which they call "the people."

Then there are spirits or ghosts. It is generally acknowledged that the best spirits come bottled. It is readily admitted that ghosts still haunt old castles and elegant homes. Irish ghosts, it seems, are fond of their comfort.

They are the inventors and international distributors of blarney. They even own the Blarney Stone. Blarney seems to be distinctive with the Irish. Like other things Irish it is difficult to describe. But you'll doubtless recognize it when you hear it!

In short, the Irish are rather glorious additions to our drab planet. Their wit is well worth a closer look, as you shall see!

J. L. K.

BLARNEY

Blarney is the secret weapon of the Irish. They have enough stock-piled to last them until Judgment Day, at which time they will all be judged by "impartial" St. Patrick and allowed into the Kingdom of Heaven, it is said.

Blarney is as old as the Irish race. It is only in relatively recent times that it acquired its own shrine in the Castle in County Cork. Each year some 70,000 blarney believers climb 120 feet in search of eloquence and hang upside down to kiss the stone. The seat of eloquence is a nondescript block of limestone about four feet long, one foot wide, and nine inches high, said to be worth about thirty million dollars.

As usual with the Irish there are many stories surrounding the stone. One is that it is Jacob's pillow brought back from the Holy Land after the Crusades.

Queen Elizabeth the First is credited with first using the word blarney. One of her henchmen in Ireland was trying, with no results, to persuade the owner of Blarney Castle to give up his ancient rights. All he delivered to the Queen was excuses, excuses, excuses. Finally the Queen in a snit screamed, "Blarney, Blarney—it's all Blarney. What he says he does not mean. What he means he does not say."

Which brings us to the definition of blarney. Maybe the queen was right. Certainly blarney is not the same as insincerity. It may deceive or flatter you but it is done without offending you. Only the Irish possess the perfect sixth sense to dispense blarney properly. It's the gift of saying the right thing rather than the obvious thing. The Irish believe that truth is too important to depend on facts.

FOLKLORE

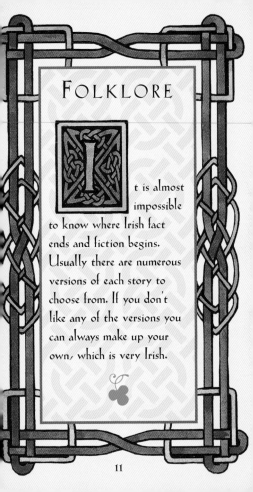

It is almost impossible to know where Irish fact ends and fiction begins. Usually there are numerous versions of each story to choose from. If you don't like any of the versions you can always make up your own, which is very Irish.

Ireland was named after an Irish Queen called Eire. Queen Eire must have had the right touch of blarney for she convinced the conquering Spanish army to name the country after her.

When the Scandinavians arrived years later they couldn't pronounce Eire so they changed the name to Ira. So it became Ira-land and the people were known as Ira-ish.

Everybody knows that St. Patrick is Ireland's patron saint. Not so well known is that he was British. He first came to Ireland not as a priest but as a young kidnapped slave. He was put to work as a shepherd for seven years before he managed to escape to France. Who knows what made him return to Ireland as a priest to convert the Irish and drive out the snakes?

It is said that before St. Patrick banished the snakes all animals could talk. Not only that, they could predict the future. Irish animals were extremely good at it.

Some people say that St. Patrick drove the snakes out of Ireland with a shamrock. Some say he used the shamrock to teach the Holy Trinity. At any rate, regardless of its use, the shamrock became the Irish national symbol in the 17th century.

St. Patrick banished all the snakes but one. He carefully lured the last snake into a box with the promise of a drink. Then he shut the box. The trapped snake pleaded with St. Patrick to let him go. St. Patrick promised to do so the following day. Instead of freeing the snake he tossed the snake, box and all, into a lake. Ever since you can hear the snake calling out, "Is this day the morrow? Is this day the morrow?"

13

Others tell the story about a huge dragon who roamed the countryside devouring women and children. St. Patrick confined him to a lake until Judgment Day. Trouble is no one is sure which lake he's in.

And then there was the colony of Irish rats that were thrown out of Ireland by a priest who used his clever tongue to charm them right into the sea. Hence Shakespeare's reference to rhyming Irish rats to death.

FAIRIES—FAIR AND FOUL

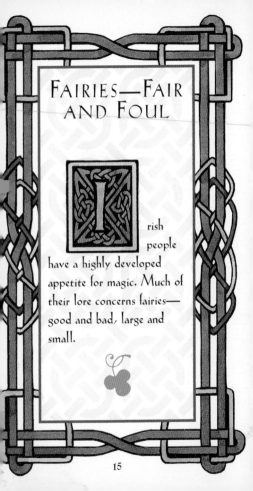

Irish people have a highly developed appetite for magic. Much of their lore concerns fairies— good and bad, large and small.

When you're in Ireland, it's wise to keep an open mind about fairies. As one Irishman put it, "I don't believe in fairies, but they're there."

No one really knows the origin of fairies. It is believed that they were the angels who revolted and were thrown out of heaven. They weren't quite bad enough to send to hell. Instead, they were sent to live forever on earth, which might account for their erratic behavior that vacillates from angelic to just plain devilish.

There are many kinds of fairies in Irish lore. Leprechauns are the working fairies. They are the tailors and cobblers. Often in the evening they can be found under a hedge stitching away at a garment or pounding a wee hammer making a pair of shoes.

Speak kindly to them if you meet one for they have the power to make you rich, providing you handle them right. First grab the Leprechaun tightly by the scruff of his neck. Be very careful not to take your eyes off him lest he disappear. Promise to let him go if he leads you to a pot of gold.

Since pots of gold are getting scarcer and scarcer these days he might arrange instead for you to win the Irish Sweepstakes.

The Pooka is a working fairy, at times. He sometimes helps with the housework but is very mischievous and combines play with work. Shakespeare, it is said, used him as the model for Puck.

The Geancanach is a very tiny fairy. He keeps his hands in his pockets and has a short pipe in his mouth at all times. He likes to stroll through lovely valleys in search of foolish country girls and make love to them. To meet him is bad luck.

The Clobher-Ceann is a mischievous fairy. He is a joking, red-faced fellow who is always found sipping from a full tankard. Beware of him for he will bring speedy ruin to you if you meet him.

Of course some people never see fairies. If you were born in the morning you won't ever see a fairy. On the other hand, if you were born at night your chances are pretty good.

One of the best times to see fairies is Halloween, when they are all out. Graves are open then and all the ghosts are out too, which tends to frighten some people.

If you see an eddy of dust it could well be a fairy dancing a jig. Fairies love music and dancing. They are said to have made the first set of pipes and danced the first Irish jig.

Fairies are extremely fond of good wine. In olden days royalty would leave a keg of wine out for them at night. It was always gone in the morning.

If you don't have wine to leave out for the fairies you can leave them a pail of water—preferably rain water. Fairies are extremely fastidious and like to bathe daily.

Fairies are frightened of fire and iron. It is well to remember this in dealing with bad fairies. Bad fairies are very mischievous. They have been known to carry off small children to raise as their own. The only way to get the child back is to swap it for a fairy child.

It is important never to leave a baby alone without taking the proper precautions. Circle the baby's cradle with a lighted candle. Fairies cannot cross a fire circle.

Fairies are said to have been conquered by a race that used iron weapons. Hence their fear of iron. Sew a tiny piece of iron in an infant's garment to protect it from the bad fairies. Hang an iron horseshoe above your door to protect your home.

In the early part of the 19th century

when superstitious practices were very common, people consulted a pishogue, a wise old woman of the village who meted out charms and incantations.

For a fee she would give a new mother something to keep the fairies out of her house for the first nine days after the birth of her baby. This gave the mother time to do all of the other tasks to insure that her child would not be kidnapped by the fairies, such as putting a prayer-book under her pillow, cutting a notch in a black cat's tail, pouring a cup of sweet milk out of the first pail when milking, or breaking a new potato on the hearthstone.

Upon first opening its eyes the infant must gaze on a blaze of candlelight to be sure it will prefer good deeds to bad.

21

Nine hairs plucked from the tail of a wild colt and bound around the baby's ankle when it is nine days old makes the baby swift and sure of foot.

There are rules to follow when going to the fair. If you meet a funeral take three steps backwards. If you meet a red-haired woman go home. If you forget something don't go back for it. If you find a white button on the road or meet a weasel you'll have good luck. Always carry some salt to protect yourself from evil.

An Irish horse is a lucky animal. He has the ability to see ghosts. It is believed that horses could talk before the great flood and can understand human speech today. Some people can gentle the wildest horses simply by whispering certain words in their ears.

So you see there is much to know about fairies, even if you don't believe in them. On the other hand, if there are no fairies how can we account for all the marvelous and magic things that happen to the Irish? Or is it just the luck of the Irish?

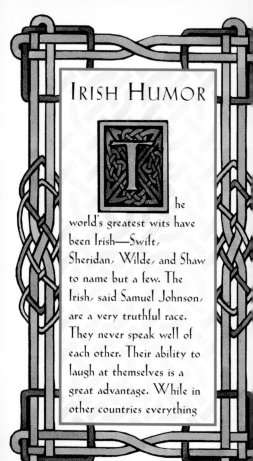

Irish Humor

The world's greatest wits have been Irish—Swift, Sheridan, Wilde, and Shaw to name but a few. The Irish, said Samuel Johnson, are a very truthful race. They never speak well of each other. Their ability to laugh at themselves is a great advantage. While in other countries everything

24

may be serious but not hopeless, in Ireland everything is hopeless but not serious.

Irish wit and humor are a national inheritance. The best Irish sayings are the sayings of the common folk. But wit and humor are common to all classes and walks of life.

Mike: That's a queer pair of stockings you have on, Pat—one red, the other green.

Pat: Yes, and I've another pair like it at home.

Mrs. Sweeney was worried about her chickens so she wrote to the Department of Agriculture:

"Dear sirs:

Every morning one or two of my chickens are lying on the ground stiff and cold with their legs in the air. I am sending two of them along to you. Could you tell me what's wrong?"

The reply was brief:

"Dear Mrs. Sweeney:

Your problem is simple. They're dead."

The priest stopped Pat on his way into church. "Pat, could you come back tomorrow for confession? We have hundreds in the church at the moment. You haven't committed a murder since last time have you?"

"Indeed no, Father. I'll come back tomorrow night."

On his way home he met Mike. "Go home Mike, and come back tomorrow. They're only hearing murderers tonight."

"I've been drinking whiskey all week to cure my sciatica."

"I can give you a better cure, Mr. Ryan."

"Shhh. I don't want to hear it."

"Bridgette, I wish you would go see how old Mrs. Murphy is this morning." Bridgette returned with the information that Mrs. Murphy was 72.

Two Irishmen driving through the country noticed that many of the barns had weather-vanes in the shape of huge roosters.

"Pat," said one man to the other, "can you tell me why they always have a rooster and never a hen on the top of those barns?"

"Sure," replied Pat, "and it must be because of the difficulty they'd have collecting the eggs."

The Irish beggar shambled over, holding out his hand. "Please give a poor blind man a dime, sir."

"But you can see out of one eye."

"Then make it a nickel."

An Irish judge charged a jury, "A man who'd maliciously set fire to a barn, and burn up a stable full of horses and mules, ought to be kicked to death by a jackass, and I'd like to be the one to do it!"

"Well, Pat, my good fellow," said a victorious general to a brave son of Erin after a battle, "and what did you do to help us gain this victory?"

"Do?" replied Pat, "May it please your honor, I walked up boldly to one of the enemy, and cut off his foot."

"Cut off his foot! And why did you not cut off his head?" asked the general.

"Ah, and faith, that was off already," says Pat.

"My lord," said the foreman of an Irish jury seriously, as he gave the verdict, "we find that the man who stole the mare is not guilty."

❧

"Ah, good morning, Mrs. Murphy, and how is everything?"

"Sure and I'm having a great time of it between my husband and the fire. If I keep my eye on the one, the other is sure to go out."

❧

Patrick had a big laugh. He saw a bull attack a man, and had to hold on to his sides with both hands, the scene was so funny. After a while the animal turned his attention in another direction, and poor Patrick, after exploring the heights, came down with a thump on the other side of the fence. He rubbed his wounds, and as he trudged along the worse for wear, he said to himself, "Faith, I'm glad I had my laugh when I did or I wouldn't have had it at all."

"Here I've been roasting over a hot stove," cried Bridget to Mike upon his return from work, "while you've been passing the day in that nice cool sewer!"

The concert hall was crowded. The Irish attendant, unable to find a seat for the pretty young miss, explained the situation to her in the following words:

"Indeed, miss, I should like to give you a seat, but the empty ones are all full."

Mrs. O'Reilly went shopping for a new suit to lay her late husband out in, for Mr. O'Reilly had departed this vale of tears only the day before. Mrs. O'Reilly had a reputation for always getting her money's worth.

"Well, and did you get him a nice new suit of clothes?" asked a neighbor, when Mrs. O'Reilly returned home.

"I sure did," was the answer. "And a bar-
gain it was, too, with an extra pair of
pants, and all."

"Drink," said the Irish preacher, "is the
greatest curse of the country. It makes you
quarrel with your neighbors. It makes you
shoot at your landlord, and it makes you
miss him."

Mike tripped and fell into a deep drain.
His companions rushed to his assistance and
found him lying motionless at the bottom.
Pat got down beside him and giving him a
shake, asked: "Are you dead, Mike?"

"No," replied Mike, "but I'm speechless."

Hearing of a friend who had a coffin
made for himself, Paddy exclaimed, "That's
a wonderful idea. It should last a lifetime."

Having accidentally broken a vase in a shop, an Irishman tried to escape. The shopkeeper grabbed him and accused him of breaking the vase and trying to run away without paying for it. "To be sure," he explained, "didn't you see me running home to get the money to pay you for it?"

A sentimental Irishman once enlisted in the 75th regiment to be near his brother who was in the 76th.

"Do you have any mementos in your locket, Mrs. Murphy?"

"A lock of my husband's hair."

"But he's still alive."

"Yes, but his hair is all gone."

"Your money or your life."

"Take my life. I'm saving my money for my old age."

Mike, pulling his wife out of a well: "Begorra a woman is at the bottom of everything."

The foreman loaded Fitzpatrick's wheelbarrow to the brim with lead piping.

Fitzpatrick scratched his head. "Would you mind, sir," he said, "tying a few concrete blocks to my ankles?"

"What for?"

"To stop me from breaking into a run."

"Paddy," jeered the tourist as he pointed to two stone dogs at either side of the entrance to an estate. "How often do you feed those dogs?"

"Every time they bark," said Paddy.

He was a small farmer who managed to live many years on ten acres and faith in the Lord. Now he was preparing to pass on to Green Pastures. He could hear the family whispering about funeral arrangements.

"Will we have two cars with the hearse?"

"Sure what do we want them for? The pony and cart will do."

"Maybe we should get a few wreaths?"

"Waste of money. We'll do without."

He struggled and sat up. "Bring me my trousers. I'll walk to the graveyard and you can cut out the hearse."

Three thugs attacked Slattery. It was a fierce struggle. Finally they got him down and took three dimes and a quarter from his pocket.

"Why did you put up a fight like that for three dimes and a quarter?" asked one of the disgusted thugs.

"Sure, I thought you were after the ten dollars in me sock," he said.

The landlady wanted to please her Irish lodger. The first day she gave him two slices of bread in his lunch. He didn't seem satisfied so she gave him four slices the next day and then six slices and finally ten. Even this wasn't enough, so, in despair, she cut the loaf in half and put the ham between the two halves.

"Had enough today, Kevin?"

"It wasn't bad," he said grudgingly, "But I see you're back to the two slices again."

Mrs. Donovan went into the confessional and was about to start when she noticed an unfamiliar face behind the shutter.

"You're not Father Geary. What are you doing here?"

"I'm the furniture polisher, Ma'am."

"Well, where is Father Geary?"

"I couldn't tell you, but if he's heard anything like the stories I've been listening to, he's gone for the police."

The maid picked up the phone and murmured something before slamming down the receiver.

"Who was that, Marie? I'm expecting a call."

"Only some idiot from Alaska. He said it was a long distance from Alaska. I told him we knew that."

The oldest inhabitant of Dublin was interviewed some years ago and was asked if he had his life to live over again, was there any major change he'd make. He thought about it.

"Indeed there is. Indeed there is," he said.

"And what would it be?"

"Sure I'd part my hair in the middle, I would."

Saloonkeeper: "Here, you haven't paid for that whiskey you ordered."

Irishman: "What's that you say?"

Saloonkeeper: "I said you haven't paid for that whiskey you ordered."

Irishman: "Did you pay for it?"

Saloonkeeper: "Of course I did."

Irishman: "Well, then, what's the good of both of us paying for it?"

She didn't approve of smoking so when the gentleman lit up his pipe she said, "Do you know that my husband is sixty and he never put a pipe in his mouth?"

"Ma'am, I'm sixty-five and never put it anywhere else."

Staggering home one night he wandered into a cemetery, tripped into a newly dug grave and fell sound asleep. Next morning when he woke up he looked around and said, "Heavens above! The day of Judgment and I'm the first up."

The three hermits had lived together for four years when one of them spoke up.

"That was a fine black horse that went by."

Three years later one of the others said, "It was a white horse."

Ten years afterwards the third member had his say. "If there's going to be bickering I won't stay."

After each drink Murphy took a frog from his pocket, put it on the bar and stared at it. Eventually the bartender asked him what he was up to.

"You see," said Murphy. "So long as I can see one frog I'm sober. It's when I see two that I have to do something."

"And what do you do?"

"I pick up the two of them, put them in my pocket and go home."

"Mr. Corrigan, I'd like to have a day off to attend my mother-in-law's funeral."

"So would I, Flynn, but she's an absolute picture of health."

The bricklayer fell twenty feet from the scaffold to the ground.

"Get him water, get him water," shouted the foreman.

The bricklayer raised himself indignantly. "And how far do you have to fall to get a drop of whiskey?"

A prisoner escaped from jail by digging a tunnel that came out in a school playground. As he crawled out of the hole he couldn't help but shout at a small girl, "I'm free. I'm free."

"That's nothing," she said scornfully, "I'm four."

They were completely drunk but when they saw the black crepe on the door they decided to go in and show respect for the dead. They tiptoed into the darkened room lit only by two candles on a grand piano. Heads down, they went over and knelt beside it, said a prayer, and tiptoed out again.

As they staggered down the street one said to the other, "I'll tell you one thing. That corpse had the finest set of teeth I ever saw."

Once there was the little boy who wanted his hair cut the same way as his daddy's—with the hole in the top for his head to come through.

And then there was the Dublin house-
holder who rushed the painting of his house
so he'd finish before the can of paint ran out.

O'Hara fell from the scaffold and
dropped two stories. His fellow workers
gathered around him and the foreman asked
him, "Did the fall hurt you?"

The victim felt his aching bones.

"It wasn't the fall hurt me. It was the
sudden stop."

It was his last confession and he didn't
want to tell a lie.

"Oh Father," he told the priest who was
attending him, "my name is Patrick
Murphy but I'm not Irish at all."

"Don't worry," consoled the priest.
"When you see St. Peter, give him your
name and then keep your mouth shut."

Paddy had a rough time with the tax inspector and couldn't make much headway. Finally, with a sigh of resignation, he suggested, "Look, why don't you keep the income and give me the tax."

They were drunk after the annual college dinner and wanted to leave the hotel.

"Look, howdjwegetout?" he asked the porter.

The porter pointed along the hall.

"Turn right at the next corner and then go down two steps and you'll be in the main hall."

They staggered on together, turned right and fell down the elevator shaft to the basement.

As they sorted themselves out Paddy said, "If that fella thinks I'm going down the other step, he's crazy."

The doctor was puzzled. Mahoney had come for a check-up and nothing seemed wrong.

"I'm very sorry but I can't diagnose your trouble, Mahoney. I think it must be drink."

"Don't worry about it, Doctor. I'll come back when you're sober."

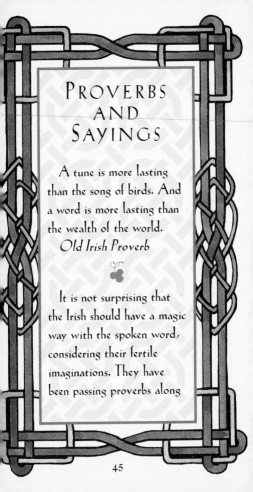

PROVERBS
AND
SAYINGS

A tune is more lasting
than the song of birds. And
a word is more lasting than
the wealth of the world.
Old Irish Proverb

It is not surprising that
the Irish should have a magic
way with the spoken word,
considering their fertile
imaginations. They have
been passing proverbs along

by word of mouth for generations now.

Each Irish village had a Seanchai, a person whose specialty was recounting memories. There were no written records in olden days. This may account for the many variations in stories. Not every Seanchai had a perfect memory.

Their tales were traditionally told to a group of people gathered around the fire. Certainly an improvement over modern day groups gathered around the TV set.

The proverbs and sayings contain more than a grain of truth and wisdom.

Always remember to forget the things that made you sad
But never forget to remember the things that made you glad.
Always remember to forget the friends that proved untrue
But don't forget to remember those that have stuck by you.

Get on your knees and thank God you're still on your feet.

Often has the likely failed and the unlikely succeeded.

Buried embers may turn to flames.

Every dog is bold at his own house door.

The whole world could not make a race horse out of a donkey.

Encourage youth and it will prosper.

A ragged colt often makes a fine horse.

The far off hills are the greenest.

Three things that are never seen are a blade's edge, the wind, and love.

A woman, a pig, and a mule are the most difficult things to teach.

There are three kinds of women: stubborn as a pig, unruly as a hen, and gentle as a lamb.

There are three kinds of men: the worker, the hunter, and the boaster.

There is not a way into the woods for which there is also not a way out of it.

The three most incomprehensible things in the world are: the mind of a woman, the labor of bees, and the ebb and flow of the tide.

There are three kinds of men who can't understand women: young men, old men, and middle-aged men.

Beware of the bull's horns, the dog's tooth, the stallion's hoof—and the Englishman's smile.

The truth from a liar is not to be believed.

Though there's no bone in a man's tongue it has frequently broken a man's head.

Every tide has its ebb.

However long the day it ends with night.

Don't let your tongue cut your throat.

Better half a loaf than no loaf at all.

Diplomacy is the ability to tell a man to go to hell so that he will look forward to the trip.

An Irishman is never drunk as long as he can hold onto one blade of grass and not fall off the face of the earth.

Death is the poor man's doctor.

A borrowed saw cuts anything.

If you want praise—die,
If you want blame—marry.

Neither make nor break a custom.

If an evil spirit pursues you at night head
for a running stream. If you can cross it
you're safe.

Be careful of the evil eye. If you see anyone staring at you through his fingers,
beware. It may be the evil eye. Immediately
say "God bless it," to break the spell.

To avoid toothaches never shave on
Sunday and never comb your hair on Friday.

To get rid of freckles dab each freckle with a bit of bull's blood.

If you wish to have a man fall in love with you offer him a drink. If he accepts (as he surely will if he's Irish) say three times to yourself:
"Thee for me
Me for thee
And for none else."

If someone is sick turn his bed so that it faces north and south with the head at the north end.

If a mad dog bites, the touch of the seventh son's hand will cure it instantly.

If you want money always carry the back tooth of a horse with you.

Wear an iron ring on the fourth finger of your left hand and you'll never have rheumatism.

Wear a crooked pin in your coat lapel for good luck in cards.

The plainest girl will be beautiful if she rises early on May Day and bathes her face in morning dew at sunrise.

A four leaf shamrock is the luckiest of all charms. If you can find one, take care never to lose it or you will lose your good luck.

IRISH SAYINGS

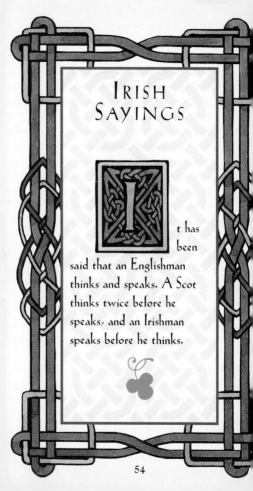

It has been said that an Englishman thinks and speaks. A Scot thinks twice before he speaks, and an Irishman speaks before he thinks.

An Englishman thinks seated, a Frenchman standing, an American pacing, and an Irishman, afterwards.

Englishman, Frenchman, Irishman!
If I weren't French I'd be English,
If I weren't English I'd be French,
If I weren't Irish I'd be ashamed.

LIMERICKS

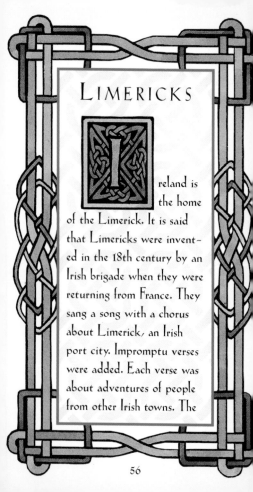

Ireland is the home of the Limerick. It is said that Limericks were invented in the 18th century by an Irish brigade when they were returning from France. They sang a song with a chorus about Limerick, an Irish port city. Impromptu verses were added. Each verse was about adventures of people from other Irish towns. The verses had to be invented on the spur of the moment, each line by a different singer. After each verse the whole group sang the chorus, "Will you come back to Limerick?" So began the Limerick.

Edward Lear introduced the Limerick to English literature with his Book of Nonsense. Lear, of course, had an Irish grandfather 'way, 'way back.

A ghost in the town of Macroom
One night found a ghoul in his room.
    They argued all night
    As to who had the right
To frighten the wits out of whom.

The puritan people of Teeling
Express all their horror with feeling.
    When they see that a chair
    Has all its legs bare,
They look straight up to the ceiling.

'Tis famous, the food of Killarney,
As tasty and fresh as sweet Blarney.
    Knowing well it is nice
    When served fast on ice,
Gourmets shriek for Chili con Kearney.

A dieting girleen named Flynn
Reduced until she was thin.
    She's no more, I'm afraid
    For she sipped lemonade,
And slipped through the straw and fell in.

Some merry old monks of Manulla
Found life was becoming much dulla.
    They brewed a fine ale,
    In a massive big pail,
And they and their lives were much fulla.

There was a young girl of Tralee
Whose knowledge of French was "oui, oui."
    Still gloriously praised
    Nightly glasses are raised
To honor her memory in Paree.

A beautiful blonde of Kilbride
Went along in a bus for the ride.
    The conductor's, "Your fare,"
    Was said with a glare.
"No, I'm not," she just grinned,
"I've been dyed."

There once were two cats of Kilkenny,
Each thought there was one cat too many;
    So they scratched and they bit,
    In a quarrelsome fit,
'Til instead of two cats there weren't any.

An ambitious girl in Kilskyre
Used paraffin lighting a fire.
> She soared into the sky,
> Without even "Goodbye,"
Now her place in the world is much higher.

An ornithological couple in Cork
Gave all of the neighbors a shock,
> With triplets galore,
> And twins by the score,
For their favorite bird was the stork.

A neurotic in old Ballindine
Lay down on a railway line.
> But it was such a bore,
> For the Four-forty-four
Didn't come 'til quarter past nine.

Cosmetically Lil of Kilquade
Had beauty that ne'er seemed to fade.
    When tanned by the sun
    She looked twenty-one,
But she looked fifty-six in the shade.

An Irishman name of Pat Sweeney
In Nice drank a quart of Martini.
    The local gendarme
    Wired his wife in alarm,
"Nous regrettons Pat Sweeney est fini."

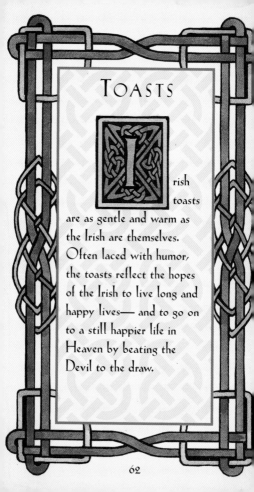

TOASTS

Irish toasts are as gentle and warm as the Irish are themselves. Often laced with humor, the toasts reflect the hopes of the Irish to live long and happy lives— and to go on to a still happier life in Heaven by beating the Devil to the draw.

May you live as long as you want
And never want as long as you live!

🍀

May the road rise up to meet you
And may the wind always be at your back
May the sun shine warm upon your face
And the raindrops fall soft upon your fields
And until we meet again
May God hold you in the small
of His hand!

🍀

Do not resist growing old—
Many are denied the privilege!

🍀

May the good Lord take a liking to you—
but not too soon!

🍀

Health and long life to you
Land without rent to you
A child every year to you
And if you can't go to Heaven
At least may you die in Ireland!

May you be in Heaven half an hour before
the Devil knows you are dead!

May there always be work
for your hands to do
May your purse always hold a coin or two
May the sun always shine on
your windowpane
May a rainbow be certain to follow each rain
May the hand of a friend always be near you
May God fill your heart with gladness—
and cheer you!

May the saddest day of the future
Be no worse than the happiest day
of the past!

As you slide down the banister of life
May the splinters never face the wrong way!